To Thanak

First published in 2013 by Blue Reamker Publishers

ISBN 978-0-9795620-2-0

Blue Reamker Publishers are editorially independent.

Many thanks to all family and friends who gave support in many ways.

Wandering Angkor

Sophie Lizeray

BLUE REAMKER

Sok Sabay!

Hello!

Join me for a trip to Angkor.

We'll be going local style, by moto of course.

Meet my faithful beat-up motorbike. Lovely isn't she!

Strap on your helmet!

Before we hit the road to Angkor, first things first : petrol stop!

A few scraps of wood nailed together and a dozen empty soda and alcohol bottles, and voilà! A neighbourhood petrol station complete with recycled containers. Stalls such as this one can be found all over town. Caught high and dry? Just look around the corner.

9

Crossing the Siem Reap river!
The river looks rather ordinary doesn't it? Well, don't be fooled by its shallow muddy waters...

This little river's source lies deep in the sacred Kulen Mountains, where King Jayavarman II founded Angkor. From the mountains, the power-charged water flows down to the Siem Reap plain. Here, ancient Khmer engineers canalized and deviated the river as early as the 10th century. They integrated it into an extensive irrigation network that once covered the kingdom of Angkor.
From Siem Reap, the river winds a few more kilometres, and ends its journey in the Tonle Sap, one of Asia's largest freshwater lakes.

So yes, this river here is quite a lady. And she must have a few tales to tell.

Welcome to the heart of the historic town, along the banks of the Siem Reap river. This is the Psar Chas, the Old Market.

The market and surrounding shop houses are abuzz with people eating, shopping, haggling, laughing and catching up on the latest gossip. Shops and cafés spill out onto the pavement, competing for space with parked motorbikes, moto drivers, shoppers and street vendors.

In the market, people dodge dangling household items, T-shirts or dried fish. They weave in and out of stalls piled precariously with nearly anything from clothes and silverware to fruits and vegetables. All around, sounds, colours and smells vie for attention.

Shop with your senses and you might stumble upon *prahok*, a pungent fermented fish paste...

Heavy traffic ahead on National Road number 6!

Running four hundred and twenty kilometres from Phnom Penh in the southeast, through Siem Reap, and all the way to the province of Banteay Meanchey in the northwest, this road is one of the longest and busiest in the country.

I wish I could trade my discreet motorbike for a 4x4 wheel-drive with a blaring horn.

Ready to squeeze our way through?

Made it!

Let's now head off the paved road onto a more peaceful laterite track.

What is laterite? It is a common surface cover in tropical Cambodia, formed by the weathering of the underlying rock. Have you noticed the ochre colour of unpaved roads? Or the reddish brown dust all over your hair and clothes after riding on trails? That's laterite.

But wait! Laterite is more than just dirt tracks. In ancient times, blocks of laterite were cut and sun-dried for construction purposes. Such blocks, along with other materials such as bamboo, timber, bricks and sandstone, were used to build Angkor's temples. Look out for their distinctive ochre colour during your visits.

The temples… laterite construction blocks… roads?

Makes you wonder… The temples of the gods are made from the same material as these dusty tracks!

Bump, bump, bump, along the countryside.

Through paddy fields, paddy fields and more paddy fields, stretching over the flat land in a profusion of green shades. From this palette, stand tall sugar palms, like upturned artist's brushes.

Farmers shade their faces with wide-brimmed hats and entwined *kramas*, Cambodian scarves. They tend to their crops, slowly wading through the shallow water, their faithful buffaloes in tow...

Buffalo crossing!

That was a close call...

Slow and steady

Mister Buffalo...

Back into the field you go!

In the countryside, the buffalo is a farmer's friend. But royalty and city folk also shower buffaloes with a lot of attention. In Phnom Penh, during the annual Chrat Preah Nongkal, Royal Ploughing festival, two buffaloes are brought to plough the sand on the ceremonial ground beside the Royal Palace.

As a reward, they are offered an array of buffalo specialities : different cereals and grains, grass, rice alcohol and water. Based on the buffaloes' choices, oracles predict the abundance of the coming year's harvest.
Now that's quite a responsibility...

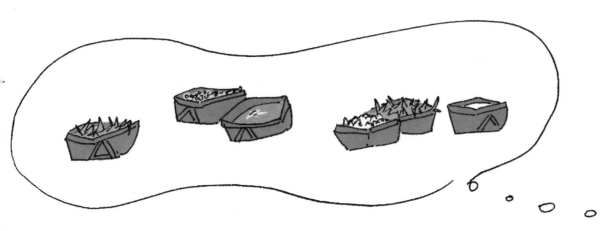

How about looking both ways before crossing a road, eh?

Look! A lotus pond!

This is *the* place to be for insects and aquatic animals. The pond provides them with shelter, food and perhaps some mating action.

Care to bring home a lotus flower as a souvenir? These beauties grow from rhizomes submerged in muddy water, and you will have to brave cold water and thorny stems to gather a few flowers and leaves. Not keen? Do not fret. The pickers' booty will find its way to the market. There you can buy lotus seeds as a snack, choose white and pink flowers for decoration and temple offerings, and perhaps carry your take-away food wrapped in waxy lotus leaves.

The trail is getting really bumpy now.
Could this be the ruins of an Angkorian road? We must be reaching the temples!

Here we are at the West Gate of Angkor Thom. The 'Great City' was founded in the late 12th century by King Jayavarman VII. Although the city itself has disappeared, the stone temples, square moat, enclosing walls and five tall gates still stand.

As we approach, the West Gate suddenly emerges from behind thick foliage, standing majestically against the jungle backdrop. Four great sculpted faces crown the doorway, each one turning to a cardinal point.

How mysterious... Could the gate be the passage between the land of man and the kingdom of the gods? I am mesmerised. Let's enter!

From the gate, the trail leads through the forest. The forest has taken over the once thriving city. It slowly decomposed, disintegrated and putrefied the timber and bamboo structures. It engulfed the city and enlaced the temples, smothering and protecting them.

Today the main temples are once again free from the forest's close embrace. But traces of the former city still lie hidden in the moisture-drenched shade of tall dipterocarps

and scrubby undergrowth. A dense network of former canals and streets remains concealed under layers of soil and plant cover. Scattered here and there, small stone ruins can also be found, perhaps fragments of ancient sacred places.

As we make our way through the forest, chirping birds, buzzing insects and singing cicadas echo the sounds of the bustling lost city. Like an invitation to travel beyond time for a fleeting instant.

Here come wood gatherers, bearing heavy loads on their back.
A timeless moment, when visitors and today's people of Angkor cross paths on a centuries-old road.

Angkor is more than just ruins and forest. It is about people and livelihoods. Angkor is a vast living canvas where past and present overlap, and man's and nature's destinies are interlaced.
Villages and modern wats dot the landscape around the temples. Farmers work in the fields and collect food and wood from the forest. They irrigate their paddy with water from modern and Angkorian canals and reservoirs. And everyone bumps along roads old and new, that crisscross on the landscape like brushstrokes.

The ancient trail we are following leads straight to the Bayon temple, at the centre of Angkor Thom. Look! We can already make out the temple's outline through the trees.

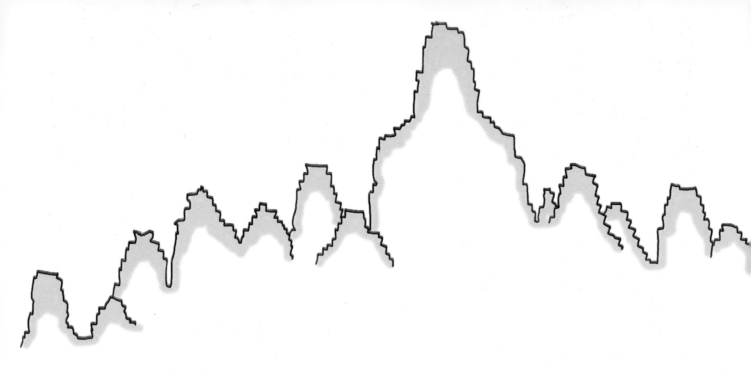

Here we are at the Bayon temple.

The Bayon was built under the reign of Buddhist King Jayavarman VII, between the late 12th and early 13th centuries. Just like sacred Mount Meru rises at the centre of the universe in Hindu and Buddhist cosmologies, the Bayon stands at the centre of the walled city of Angkor Thom.

The temple mountain is built on three levels. At the centre of the highest terrace, the main sanctuary offers its pinnacle to the sky. A forest of towers surrounds it, each crowned by gigantic sculpted faces. As we approach, their features slowly become more and more distinct.

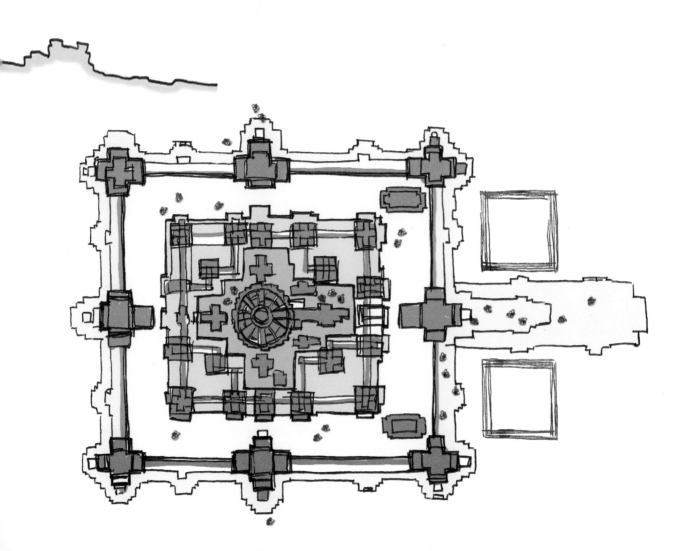

Let's enter the Bayon and walk along the outer gallery.
Bas-reliefs cover the walls, sometimes almost spilling over the edges. The stones are alive with historic events and scenes from everyday life. They tell captivating and exuberant stories, precious testimonies of life in Angkorian times.

Here, fishermen jostle with farmers and princes. There, merchants strike a deal, cooks prepare a feast and soldiers get ready for battle. Further away, trees spread their branches to the limits of their stone frame. And here come animals! Elephants, birds, fish, spring out from every crack in the stone.

Up and down through the Bayon's labyrinthine galleries and levels. From light to shadow and back to light... One last stepped passageway and here we are on the top terrace, an instant blinded by the sudden daylight.
Slowly, blinking, I realize I am staring at colossal faces, their features carved into stone blocks. Up-close, the stone's rough surface seems to breathe like the pores of the skin. Every crack becomes a wrinkle, and every crevice a scar.

With frozen smiles and inscrutable expressions, the faces appear to acknowledge one another. And although their eyes are closed, their gaze seems to follow our every move.

Whose are these mysterious faces? What are they saying?

Are they symbols of the omniscient, ever-present Buddha?

Are they portraits of Jayavarman VII embracing all four corners of his kingdom with his powerful gaze?

No matter what they are, these faces have been scanning the land for over eight hundred years, observing in silence as time passes by.
I wonder what they see today, and what they think of our world.

Daydreaming...
A forest of stone giants, with kind gazes and serene smiles...

42

In the blink of an eye, their features twist into oppressive snarls.

And just as suddenly, unfurl into the same mysterious smiles with placid impenetrable eyes.

One moment I am still in a daze, and the next I am surrounded by a swarm of children, peddling small souvenirs and all shouting gleefully.

« Bong Srei! Bong Srei! Elder Sister! You buy something, Bong Srei!
How much are the postcards?
One dollar, Bong Srei!
How old are you?
Eight years old, Bong Srei! »

Five, eight, twelve...
Elder Sister, foreigner, tourist, wealthier...

What lies behind the children's bright eyes and chirpy laughter? How many packets of postcards or little bracelets can I buy to make a difference?
Sometimes I feel more helpless than hopeful, sometimes more hopeful than helpless.
Perhaps, if the energy and resilience of Angkor's young vendors is anything to go by, there is hope that they can make the most out of life's challenges.

Quiet pondering.
Wandering, wondering.

Shall we head on?

Let's exit the ancient city of Angkor Thom by the South Gate. Two rows of mythical creatures, the Giants and the Demons, are lined up to bid us farewell.

Or are they?

What are they tugging at?
It is Naga's body, the sacred serpent! We have just stumbled upon the Churning of the Milk Ocean.

According to Hindu mythology, the Giants and the Demons once lost the nectar of immortality. Together, they churned the Milk Ocean with Naga's body, in the hope of making the precious elixir reappear. The churning lasted a thousand years. At last, the treasured nectar materialized, but the Giants and the Demons fought over it... and lost it again.

Hurry! Let's leave them to their cosmic conspiracies...

… and make our way to Angkor Wat instead.

Stone lions glare down at us intimidatingly as we enter the great causeway. They stand guard, proudly protecting the western entrance of Angkor Wat. With bared teeth and rolling eyeballs, they look ferociously poised to leap out of their stone shells.

Angkor Wat was built in the early 12th century, under the reign of Suryavarman II. His new capital was designed to represent the universe, where oceans and mountains surround the sacred Mount Meru.

Angkor Wat is enclosed by a square moat, representing the oceans. Inside the moat once lay the city itself, protected by walls and galleries, said to embody high mountain chains. Here, a myriad of legendary heroes and celestial beings - Apsaras and Devatas - are carefully chiselled into the stone. At the centre of Angkor Wat, five towers, symbols of Mount Meru's five peaks, rise over the prodigious mountains and oceans. The tallest tower houses the temple's inner sanctuary.

Oceans, mountains and mythological creatures... These great obstacles await those wishing to reach the gods' abode!

My favourite sanctuary in Angkor Wat today does not lie at the top of the temple's highest pinnacle. It is right here, by the West Gate. Please take your shoes off and come meet an impressive eight-armed Vishnu!

People gather here to pray and chat. They lay out offerings, burn joss sticks or squeeze a few bills into the donation box.

But why is this representation of Vishnu still worshiped today in a predominantly Buddhist country?

Angkor Wat was at first dedicated to Vishnu. Later, in the 13th century, Buddhism became the country's official religion, and Buddha images made their appearance in Angkor Wat alongside sculptures of Hindu deities. But there is more to this mighty statue. It is also known as Ta Reach, and is said to house the most powerful Neak Ta - the spirit of a place - in the entire Angkor region.

Part Vishnu, part Buddha, part Neak Ta... Let's light a few joss sticks and ask him to watch over Angkor for many more years to come.

And now, before leaving Angkor, let's enjoy the sunset by the moat.

Water, forest, stone.
Ancient kingdoms and today's city.

Light and shadow
Stone faces, real people
Mountains, myths, magic
Dirt roads and star dust.

Sunset over Angkor.

Hello?

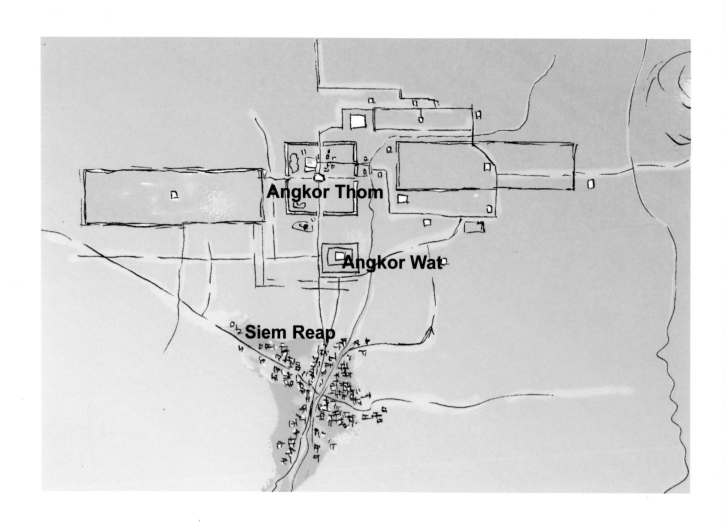

Angkor Thom

Angkor Wat

Siem Reap

About the author :

Sophie Lizeray grew up in Asia and later moved to Europe.
Life then brought her back to Asia, and back to Europe, and back to Asia...

She first visited Cambodia in 1999, and returned to live and work.

Sophie is a landscape architect, a yoga teacher and a mother.

Follow her on
www.fissosworld.com

Beep! Beep!